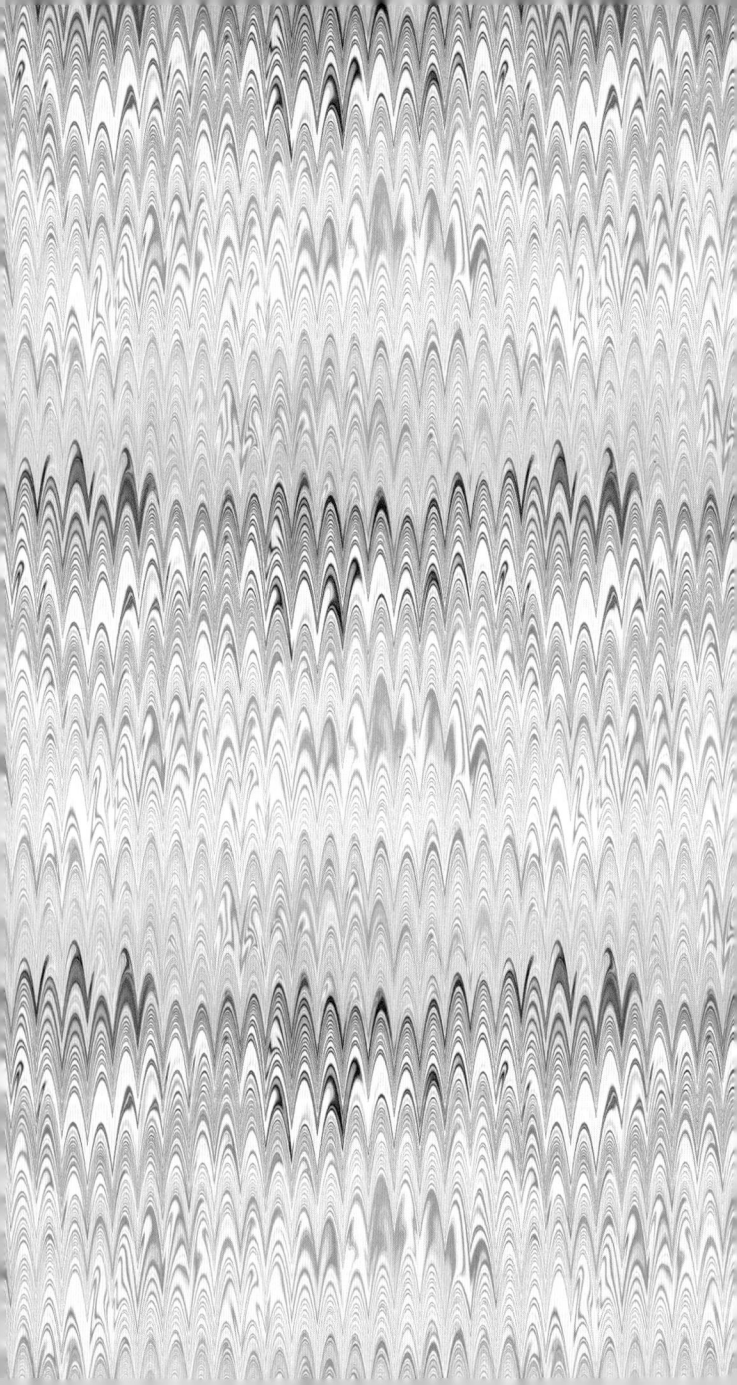

RULES OF CIVILITY
AND DECENT BEHAVIOR
IN COMPANY AND CONVERSATION

&

GEORGE WASHINGTON'S
FIRST INAUGURAL
ADDRESS

PETER PAUPER PRESS, INC.
Rye Brook, New York

PETER PAUPER PRESS
Fine Books and Gifts Since 1928

Our Company

In 1928, at the age of twenty-two, Peter Beilenson began printing books on a small press in the basement of his parents' home in Larchmont, New York. Peter—and later, his wife, Edna—sought to create fine books that sold at "prices even a pauper could afford."

Today, still family owned and operated, Peter Pauper Press continues to honor our founders' legacy—and our customers' expectations—of beauty, quality, and value.

Designed by Margaret Rubiano

Cover image © Paper Element via Creative Market
Endsheet and other images used under license from Shutterstock.com

This edition copyright © 2024
Peter Pauper Press, Inc.
3 International Drive
Rye Brook, NY 10573 USA

Library of Congress Control Number: 2023951430

All rights reserved
ISBN 978-1-4413-4351-2
Printed in China

7 6 5 4 3 2 1

Visit us at www.peterpauper.com

CONTENTS

Rules of Civility and Decent
Behavior in Company and
Conversation 7

George Washington's
First Inaugural Address 49

❋ ❋ ❋

ONE OF GEORGE WASHINGTON'S EARLIEST known manuscripts is *Rules of Civility*, which dates to 1745. This manuscript is not a list of rules our first president came up with himself; rather, the rules in this book are the result of a writing exercise. At around fourteen or fifteen years of age, Washington most likely copied, from a late sixteenth-century French etiquette manual, instructions for living in polite society.

Washington copied 110 of those instructions nearly two hundred years after the manual was published, and its enclosed directives are now considered an early and enduring influence on his character. Although it's been almost three hundred years since Washington transcribed them, many of the rules still hold true today. Often, they stress the importance of humility and sincerity. They recommend submitting judgement with modesty, withholding unasked-for advice, and taking important events and experiences seriously. And while the advice to not spit in fires no longer guides us at the dinner table, the instructions for hosting and being a good guest remain valuable when we consider how we move through the world.

Other maxims included in the manuscript have to do with authority, stressing the importance of knowing one's superiors and how to conduct oneself in both formal and informal company. Not all of these instructions necessarily match the social and political landscape of our time. Perhaps instead, we can consider how these rules, painstakingly copied in Washington's teenage cursive, reveal the conventions that governed Europe and colonial America. They tell us about our country's history.

Looking back, we can get a better sense of the culture that shaped Washington and some of the ways that culture has changed, in part, as a result of his personal and political life. Washington ended his exercise with a reminder to keep alive the "little spark of celestial fire called conscience," a message that still resonates today.

Rules of Civility and Decent Behavior in Company and Conversation

Every action done in company ought to be with some sign of respect to those that are present.

✻ ✻ ✻

When in company, put not your hands to any part of the body not usually discovered.

✻ ✻ ✻

Show nothing to your friend that may affright him.

In the presence of others, sing not to yourself with a humming noise, nor drum with your fingers or feet.

If you cough, sneeze, sigh, or yawn, do it not loud but privately; and speak not in your yawning, but put your handkerchief or hand before your face and turn aside.

Sleep not when others speak, sit not when others stand, speak not when you should hold your peace, walk not on when others stop.

Put not off your clothes in the presence of others, nor go out your chamber half dressed.

At play and at fire, it's good manners to give place to the last comer, and affect not to speak louder than ordinary.

Spit not in the fire, nor stoop low before it.
Neither put your hands into the flames
to warm them, nor set your feet upon the fire,
especially if there be meat before it.

10.

When you sit down, keep your feet firm and even,
without putting one on the other or crossing them.

11.

Shift not yourself in the sight of others
nor gnaw your nails.

12.

Shake not the head, feet, or legs; roll not the eyes,
lift not one eyebrow higher than the other;
wry not the mouth, and bedew no man's face
with your spittle by approaching too near
him when you speak.

13.

Kill no vermin as fleas, lice, ticks, etc. in the sight of
others. If you see any filth or thick spittle, put your foot
dexterously upon it; if it be upon the clothes of your
companions, put it off privately, and if it be upon your
own clothes, return thanks to him who puts it off.

14.

Turn not your back to others, especially
in speaking; jog not the table or desk on which
another reads or writes; lean not upon anyone.

15.

Keep your nails clean and short, also your
hands and teeth clean, yet without showing any
great concern for them.

16.

Do not puff up the cheeks, loll not out the tongue,
rub the hands, or beard, thrust out the lips,
or bite them, or keep the lips too open or too close.

Be no flatterer, neither play with any that
delights not to be played with.

18.

Read no letters, books, or papers in company,
but when there is a necessity for the doing of it
you must ask leave. Come not near the books or
writings of another so as to read them, unless desired,
or give your opinion of them unasked.
Also look not nigh when another is writing a letter.

19.

Let your countenance be pleasant, but in
serious matters somewhat grave.

The gestures of the body must be suited
to the discourse you are upon.

Reproach none for the infirmities of nature,
nor delight to put them that have in mind thereof.

Show not yourself glad at the misfortune
of another, though he were your enemy.

23.

When you see a crime punished, you may be inwardly
pleased, but always show pity to the suffering offender.

24.

Do not laugh too loud or too much
at any public spectacle.

25.

Superfluous compliments and all affectation
of ceremony are to be avoided, yet where due they
are not to be neglected.

26.

In pulling off your hat to persons of distinction,
as noblemen, justices, churchmen, etc., make
a reverence, bowing more or less according to the
custom of the better bred, and quality of the person.
Amongst your equals, expect not always that they
should begin with you first, but to pull off the hat
when there is no need is affectation; in the manner
of saluting and resaluting in words, keep to
the most usual custom.

27.

'Tis ill manners to bid one more eminent than yourself
be covered as well as not to do it to whom it's due.
Likewise, he that makes too much haste to put on his hat
does not well, yet he ought to put it on at the first, or at
most the second time of being asked. Now what is herein
spoken, of qualification in behavior in saluting, ought
also to be observed in taking of place, and sitting down
for ceremonies without bounds is troublesome.

28.

If anyone come to speak to you while you are sitting, stand up though he be your inferior, and when you present seats, let it be to everyone according to his degree.

29.

When you meet with one of greater quality than yourself, stop, and retire, especially if it be at a door or any straight place to give way for him to pass.

30.

In walking, the highest place in most countries seems to be on the right hand, therefore place yourself on the left of him whom you desire to honor: but if three walk together, the mid place is the most honorable; the wall is usually given to the most worthy if two walk together.

31.

If anyone far surpasses others, either in age, estate, or merit, yet would give place to a meaner than himself in his own lodging or elsewhere, the one ought not to accept it, so he on the other part should not use much earnestness nor offer it above once or twice.

32.

To one that is your equal, or not much inferior, you are to give the chief place in your lodging, and he to who it is offered ought at the first to refuse it, but at the second to accept, though not without acknowledging his own unworthiness.

33.

They that are in dignity or in office have in all places precedency, but whilst they are young they ought to respect those that are their equals in birth or other qualities, though they have no public charge.

34.

It is good manners to prefer them to whom
we speak before ourselves, especially if they be above
us with whom in no sort we ought to begin.

35.

Let your discourse with men of business
be short and comprehensive.

36.

Artificers & persons of low degree ought not
to use many ceremonies to lords, or others of high
degree, but respect and highly honor them, and
those of high degree ought to treat them with
affability & courtesy, without arrogancy.

37.

In speaking to men of quality, do not lean nor look them full in the face, nor approach too near them; at least keep a full pace from them.

※ ※ ※

38.

In visiting the sick, do not presently play the physician if you be not knowing therein.

※ ※ ※

39.

In writing or speaking, give to every person his due title according to his degree & the custom of the place.

※ ※ ※

40.

Strive not with your superiors in argument, but always submit your judgment to others with modesty.

41.

Undertake not to teach your equal in the art himself professes; it savors of arrogancy.

42.

Let thy ceremonies in courtesy be proper to the dignity of his place with whom thou converses, for it is absurd to act the same with a clown and a prince.

43.

Do not express joy before one sick or in pain, for that contrary passion will aggravate his misery.

44.

When a man does all he can, though it succeeds not well, blame not him that did it.

45.

Being to advise or reprehend anyone, consider whether it ought to be in public or in private; presently, or at some other time, in what terms to do it; & in reproving show no sign of choler, but do it with all sweetness and mildness.

46.

Take all admonitions thankfully in what time or place soever given, but afterwards, not being culpable, take a time & place convenient to let him know it that gave them.

47.

Mock not nor jest at anything of importance,
break no jest that are sharp biting, and if you deliver
anything witty and pleasant, abstain from laughing
thereat yourself.

✳ ✳ ✳

48.

Wherein you reprove another, be unblameable yourself,
for example is more prevalent than precepts.

✳ ✳ ✳

49.

Use no reproachful language against anyone;
neither curse nor revile.

✳ ✳ ✳

Be not hasty to believe flying reports to the disparagement of any.

* * *

Wear not your clothes foul, unripped, or dusty, but see they be brushed once every day at least, and take heed that you approach not to any uncleanness.

* * *

In your apparel be modest and endeavor to accommodate nature; rather than to procure admiration, keep to the fashion of your equals, such as are civil and orderly with respect to times and places.

* * *

Run not in the streets, neither go too slowly, nor with mouth open; go not shaking your arms, kick not the earth with your feet; go not upon the toes, nor in a dancing fashion.

※ ※ ※

Play not the peacock, looking everywhere about you to see if you be well decked, if your shoes fit well, if your stockings sit neatly, and clothes handsomely.

※ ※ ※

Eat not in the streets, nor in the house, out of season.

※ ※ ※

Associate yourself with men of good quality if you esteem your own reputation; for it is better to be alone than in bad company.

In walking up and down in a house, only with one in company if he be greater than yourself, at the first give him the right hand and stop not till he does, and be not the first that turns, and when you do turn let it be with your face towards him; if he be a man of great quality, walk not with him cheek by jowl but somewhat behind him, but yet in such a manner that he may easily speak to you.

58.

Let your conversation be without malice or envy,
for it is a sign of a tractable and commendable nature;
and in all causes of passion admit reason to govern.

59.

Never express anything unbecoming, nor act against
the rules moral before your inferiors.

60.

Be not immodest in urging your friends
to discover a secret.

61.

Utter not base and frivolous things amongst grave
and learned men; nor very difficult questions
or subjects among the ignorant; or things hard to be
believed, stuff not your discourse with sentences
amongst your betters nor equals.

62.

Speak not of doleful things in a time of mirth
or at the table; speak not of melancholy things
as death and wounds, and if others mention them,
change if you can the discourse; tell not your dreams,
but to your intimate friend.

A man ought not to value himself of his achievements, or rare qualities of wit, much less of his riches, virtue or kindred.

Break not a jest where none take pleasure in mirth; laugh not aloud, nor at all without occasion; deride no man's misfortune, though there seem to be some cause.

Speak not injurious words, neither in jest nor earnest; scoff at none, although they give occasion.

66.

Be not froward but friendly and courteous;
be the first to salute, hear, and answer; & be not
pensive when it's a time to converse.

67.

Detract not from others; neither be excessive
in commanding.

68.

Go not thither where you know not whether you
shall be welcome or not. Give not advice without being
asked & when desired do it briefly.

69.

If two contend together, take not the part of either unconstrained; and be not obstinate in your own opinion; in things indifferent be of the major side.

70.

Reprehend not the imperfections of others, for that belongs to parents, masters, and superiors.

71.

Gaze not on the marks or blemishes of others and ask not how they came. What you may speak in secret to your friend, deliver not before others.

72.

Speak not in an unknown tongue in company, but in your own language and that as those of quality do and not as the vulgar. Sublime matters treat seriously.

* * *

73.

Think before you speak, pronounce not imperfectly, nor bring out your words too hastily, but orderly & distinctly.

* * *

74.

When another speaks, be attentive yourself and disturb not the audience; if any hesitate in his words, help him not nor prompt him without desired, interrupt him not, nor answer him till his speech be ended.

* * *

75.

In the midst of discourse ask not of what one treateth, but if you perceive any stop because of your coming you may well entreat him gently to proceed. If a person of quality comes in while you're conversing, it's handsome to repeat what was said before.

76.

While you are talking, point not with your finger at him of whom you discourse nor approach too near him to whom you talk, especially to his face.

Treat with men at fit times about business & whisper not in the company of others.

Make no comparisons, and if any of the company be commended for any brave act of virtue, commend not another for the same.

Be not apt to relate news if you know not the truth thereof. In discoursing of things you have heard, name not your author; always a secret discover not.

80.

Be not tedious in discourse or in reading unless you find the company pleased therewith.

81.

Be not curious to know the affairs of others; neither approach those that speak in private.

82.

Undertake not what you cannot perform, but be careful to keep your promise.

When you deliver a matter, do it without passion & with discretion, however mean the person be you do it to.

When your superiors talk to any body, hearken not, neither speak nor laugh.

In company of those of higher quality than yourself, speak not till you are asked a question, then stand upright, put off your hat, & answer in few words.

In disputes, be not so desirous to overcome as not to give liberty to each one to deliver his opinion and submit to the judgment of the major part, especially if they are judges of the dispute.

Let thy carriage be such as becomes a man grave, settled, and attentive to that which is spoken. Contradict not at every turn what others say.

Be not tedious in discourse, make not many digressions, nor repeat often the same manner of discourse.

89.

Speak not evil of the absent, for it is unjust.

90.

Being set at meat, scratch not, neither spit, cough, or blow your nose, except if there's a necessity for it.

91.

Make no show of taking great delight in your victuals; feed not with greediness, cut your bread with a knife, lean not on the table, neither find fault with what you eat.

92.

Take no salt or cut bread with your knife greasy.

⁂

93.

Entertaining anyone at table, it is decent to present him with meat; undertake not to help others undesired by the master.

⁂

94.

If you soak bread in the sauce, let it be no more than what you put in your mouth at a time; and blow not your broth at table, but stay till it cools of itself.

⁂

95.

Put not your meat to your mouth with your knife in your hand; neither spit forth the stones of any fruit pie upon a dish nor cast anything under the table.

96.

It's unbecoming to stoop much to one's meat; keep your fingers clean, & when foul, wipe them on a corner of your table napkin.

97.

Put not another bit into your mouth till the former be swallowed; let not your morsels be too big for the jowls.

98.

Drink not nor talk with your mouth full; neither gaze about you while you are drinking.

※ ※ ※

99.

Drink not too leisurely nor yet too hastily; before and after drinking, wipe your lips; breathe not then or ever with too great a noise, for it's uncivil.

※ ※ ※

100.

Cleanse not your teeth with the tablecloth, napkin, fork, or knife, but if others do it, let it be done with a picktooth.

※ ※ ※

101.

Rinse not your mouth in the presence of others.

102.

It is out of use to call upon the company often to eat, nor need you drink to others every time you drink.

103.

In company of your betters, be not longer in eating than they are; lay not your arm but only your hand upon the table.

104.

It belongs to the chiefest in company to unfold his napkin and fall to meat first, but he ought then to begin in time & to dispatch with dexterity that the slowest may have time allowed him.

105.

Be not angry at table whatever happens, & if you have reason to be so, show it not but put on a cheerful countenance, especially if there be strangers, for good humor makes one dish of meat a feast.

106.

Set not yourself at the upper end of the table, but if it be your due or that the master of the house will have it so, contend not, lest you should trouble the company.

107.

If others talk at table, be attentive, but talk not with meat in your mouth.

108.

When you speak of God or his attributes, let it be seriously & with reverence. Honor & obey your natural parents although they be poor.

109.

Let your recreations be manful, not sinful.

110.

Labor to keep alive in your breast that little spark of celestial fire called conscience.

George Washington's First Inaugural Address

April 30, 1789

Fellow Citizens of the Senate and the House of Representatives:

Among the vicissitudes incident to life, no event could have filled me with greater anxieties than that of which the notification was transmitted by your order, and received on the fourteenth day of the present month. On the one hand, I was summoned by my Country, whose voice I can never hear but with veneration and love, from a retreat which I had chosen with the fondest predilection, and, in my flattering hopes, with an immutable decision, as the asylum of my declining years: a retreat which was rendered every day more necessary as well as more dear to me, by the addition of habit to inclination, and of frequent interruptions in my health to the gradual waste committed on it by time. On the other hand, the magnitude and difficulty of the trust to which the voice of my Country called me, being sufficient to awaken in the wisest and most experienced of her citizens, a distrustful scrutiny into his qualifications, could not but overwhelm with despondence, one, who, inheriting inferior endowments from nature and unpracticed in the duties of civil administration, ought to be peculiarly

conscious of his own deficiencies. In this conflict of emotions, all I dare aver, is, that it has been my faithful study to collect my duty from a just appreciation of every circumstance, by which it might be affected. All I dare hope, is, that, if in executing this task I have been too much swayed by a grateful remembrance of former instances, or by an affectionate sensibility to this transcendent proof, of the confidence of my fellow-citizens; and have thence too little consulted my incapacity as well as disinclination for the weighty and untried cares before me; my error will be palliated by the motives which misled me, and its consequences be judged by my Country, with some share of the partiality in which they originated.

Such being the impressions under which I have, in obedience to the public summons, repaired to the present station; it would be peculiarly improper to omit in this first official Act, my fervent supplications to that Almighty Being who rules over the Universe, who presides in the Councils of Nations, and whose providential aids can supply every human defect, that his benediction may consecrate to the liberties and happiness of the People of the United States, a Government instituted by themselves for these essential purposes: and may enable every instrument employed in its administration to execute with success, the functions allotted to his charge. In tendering this homage to the Great Author of every public and private good I assure myself that it expresses your sentiments not less than my own; nor those of my fellow-citizens at large, less than either. No People can be bound to acknowledge and adore the invisible hand, which conducts the Affairs of men, more than the People of the United States. Every step, by which they have advanced to the character of an independent nation, seems to have been distinguished by some token of providential agency. And in the important revolution just accomplished in the system of their United Government, the tranquil deliberations and voluntary consent of so many distinct communities, from which the event has resulted, cannot be compared with the means by which most Governments have been established, without some return of pious gratitude along with a humble anticipation of the future blessings which the past seem to presage. These reflections, arising out of the present crisis, have forced themselves too strongly on my mind to be suppressed. You will join with me I trust in thinking, that there are none under the influence of which, the proceedings of a new and free Government can more auspiciously commence.

By the article establishing the Executive Department, it is made the duty of the President "to recommend to your consideration, such measures as he shall judge necessary and expedient." The circumstances under which I now meet you, will acquit me from entering into that subject, farther than to refer to the Great Constitutional Charter under which you are assembled; and which, in defining your powers, designates the objects to which your attention is to be given. It will be more consistent with those circumstances, and far more congenial with the feelings which actuate me, to substitute, in place of a recommendation of particular measures, the tribute that is due to the talents, the rectitude, and the patriotism which adorn the characters selected to devise and adopt them. In these honorable qualifications, I behold the surest pledges, that as on one side, no local prejudices, or attachments; no separate views, nor party animosities, will misdirect the comprehensive and equal eye which ought to watch over this great assemblage of communities and interests: so, on another, that the foundations of our National policy will be laid in the pure and immutable principles of private morality; and the pre-eminence of a free Government, be exemplified by all the attributes which can win the affections of its Citizens, and command the respect of the world.

I dwell on this prospect with every satisfaction which an ardent love for my Country can inspire: since there is no truth more thoroughly established, than that there exists in the economy and course of nature, an indissoluble union between virtue and happiness, between duty and advantage, between the genuine maxims of an honest and magnanimous policy, and the solid rewards of public prosperity and felicity: Since we ought to be no less persuaded that the propitious smiles of Heaven, can never be expected on a nation that disregards the eternal rules of order and right, which Heaven itself has ordained: And since the preservation of the sacred fire of liberty, and the destiny of the Republican model of Government, are justly considered as deeply, perhaps as finally staked, on the experiment entrusted to the hands of the American people.

Besides the ordinary objects submitted to your care, it will remain with your judgment to decide, how far an exercise of the occasional power delegated by the Fifth article of the Constitution is rendered expedient at the present juncture by the nature of objections which have been urged against the System, or by the degree of inquietude which has given birth to them. Instead of undertaking particular recommendations on this subject, in which I could be guided by no lights derived from official opportunities, I shall again give way to my entire confidence in your discernment and pursuit of the public good: For I assure myself that whilst you carefully avoid every alteration which might endanger the benefits of a United and effective Government, or which ought to await the future lessons of experience; a reverence for the characteristic rights of freemen, and a regard for the public harmony, will sufficiently influence your deliberations on the question how far the former can be more impregnably fortified, or the latter be safely and advantageously promoted.

To the preceding observations I have one to add, which will be most properly addressed to the House of Representatives. It concerns myself, and will therefore be as brief as possible. When I was first honored with a call into the Service of my Country, then on the eve of an arduous struggle for its liberties, the light in which I contemplated my duty required that I should renounce every pecuniary compensation. From this resolution I have in no instance departed. And being still under the impressions which produced it, I must decline as inapplicable to myself, any share in the personal emoluments, which may be indispensably included in a permanent provision for the Executive Department; and must accordingly pray that the pecuniary estimates for the Station in which I am placed, may, during my continuance in it, be limited to such actual expenditures as the public good may be thought to require.

Having thus imported to you my sentiments, as they have been awakened by the occasion which brings us together, I shall take my present leave; but not without resorting once more to the benign parent of the human race, in humble supplication that since he has been pleased to favor the American people, with opportunities for deliberating in perfect tranquility, and dispositions for deciding with unparalleled unanimity on a form of Government, for the security of their Union, and the advancement of their happiness; so his divine blessing may be equally conspicuous in the enlarged views, the temperate consultations, and the wise measures on which the success of this Government must depend.

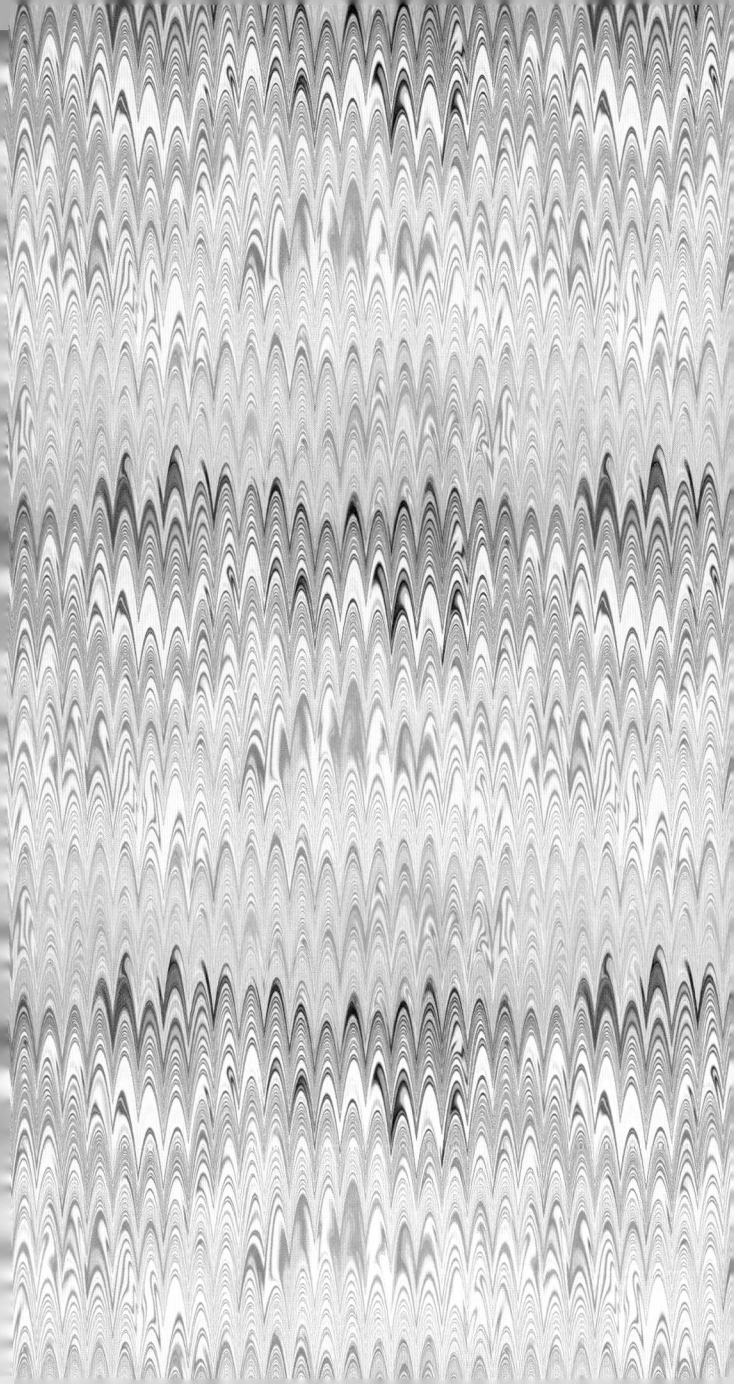